GREEK ISLAND ADVENTURES

Escapades for the Sophisticated Traveler

Claudia Kielich

Contents

Introduction	vii
1. MY MOTHER, A TRUE GODDESS	1
2. AIRPLANE TO GREECE	3
3. MAGDA	7
4. KOSTAS & SOULA	15
5. THALIA	21
6. IRINI	25
7. MARIA & ALESSANDRA	31
8. MELINA MERCOURI	35
9. ATHENA	39
10. KATERINA	43
11. YIANNIS & ANASTASIA	47
12. VASILIKI	51
13. TEMPLE OF APHAIA	55
GREEK FAMILY RECIPES	59
About the Author	81

*Dedicated to my family Spiros, Chantal, and Theodore
For all of their love and support*

Introduction

This is a book of heartfelt short stories for the Traveler and the Armchair Traveler featuring Greece and the Greek Islands, where every intoxicating story showcases lively characters and their life experiences through the author, Claudia Kielich, a world traveler, who has spent over 20 years traveling the Greek Islands.

It reads like a travelogue for everyone who fantasizes about Greece with its tantalizing homemade food, the sensual pleasure of a morning swim in the Mediterranean, the welcoming landscapes of the Peloponnese, and most of all the unforgettable people. Readers say it's a great read and a great ride.

Adventures in the book include titillating stories that are the outcome of exploration and research for her business, Goddesses Go To Greece Adventure Travel, that introduces the reader to such characters as Thalia, who built her own hotel out of rocks from the sea and the road on Lemnos; two aristocrats, Maria and Alessandra, who share their magical past in Athens; Irini, who owns a lovely cliff hotel on the island of Amorgos where she hosts Greek cooking classes in her garden of island grown herbs, by day, and unlimited village fun by night; Yiannis and Anastasia who offer a hilarious tour of the secret cafes of Crete; and story after story. As a final treat the book ends with the thrilling story of the awakening experience on Aegina, alone in the Temple Aphaia, with a stranger from a far off land.

Chapter 1
MY MOTHER, A TRUE GODDESS

One of the reasons I created a unique travel business for women, "Goddesses Go to Greece" is my childhood. Growing up in Buffalo, New York, with six months a year of cold and snow, my mother of seven children certainly had her challenges. When we were all very young she would dress us and undress us for our outdoor play and when I think of it now, just the idea of seven children going in and out in the cold wet snow asking to warm up and then getting all dressed again to go out umpteen times a day, I don't know how she did it.

However, my mother was a Goddess. A Goddess who took off twice a year to a Catholic Retreat House in upstate New York for a week at a time, where she would listen to fabulous music, lectures and eat nutritious food and experience hours of silence, which I am sure she relished. She had no problem leaving all of us kids with our father and whomever he could dig up to help him out. My mother and her friends had more freedom to escape the family and travel alone than women do today.

Why is it that the modern woman feels so guilty if she has fun or if she even desires fun. It's like a dark secret we keep to ourselves and rarely share with our female friends. I believe it is why when we go through empty nesting and later our self transition, we have nowhere to go inside because we have kept that door locked for so long. God forbid we mention we would like to take off on a vacation alone to replenish, refresh, rejuvenate and find our inner Goddess.

The women in Greece remind me of my mother, whom I believe to be Goddess Artemis. Greek women do everything with such grace and save any expression of their disappointments or frustrations for their close women friends. They know how to share and not to pretend with one another that everything is great. Because of this, the friendships are deep and lifelong. You can see it in their faces when they greet each other and when they eat and drink with each other. This is a Grecian festivity on an ongoing basis. I am lucky to participate whenever I am invited to these soirees of Goddess Gossip and Girls Just Having Fun! What a concept. We know in our hearts we love our family and friends, but at times we do need to let off some steam and why not do it sipping ouzo sitting at a table in the sea on a Greek Island. Our favorite place to swim, sun and sip.

This is my journey. . . to find my Inner Goddess.

Chapter 2

AIRPLANE TO GREECE

He was curled up at the window when I arrived, prepared to sleep and perhaps looking for silence. I am thrilled that the overnight flight to Athens will be comfortable since I can tell he is small like me and won't be squeezing me for the armrest. I have a sudden urge to bother this man with an outburst of thank heavens that we're both small. Later he shared with me, as a Cretan, the reason Greek names end in "is" is because the word means small and the Turks wanted to humiliate the Greeks after they conquered them.

Marcos is his name and once I shared with him my good humor and desire to create a tour to Crete for Goddesses Go to Greece; he is now smiling that he met me. We choose to relax and set our seats back and he begins with a wonderful smile that reminds me of a Greek Sean Penn. Marcos is on his way to check on his 1200 olive trees that he owns that were handed down for generations in his family. He shares that he is unusual for his small size since men from Crete were sent first to fight the Turks because of their unusually large size. But that's okay, to me he is larger than life, since he has a long list of things for me to view on Crete and people for me to meet. Together we design a trip of a lifetime for anyone who wants to see Crete through a Cretan's eyes.

I will begin my Cretan tour in Chania, the capital, where the harbor dictates the way of life as very classy, with art, food, museums and an enthusiastic population ready to greet newcomers.

Outside Chania, to the east, the villages of Vamos and Doyliania, are the most traditional on the island. Here I will taste the best cheeses that Marcos describes as heavenly. Mizithra, Antthotiros, Maana, Hefalotiri, Feta, and then move on to the chamomile tea. We eat our dinner and then doze off after two movies, and to my surprise, when I awake he is crossing his leg with his foot toward me, pulling up the ankle of his pants to reveal a tattoo of Crete. Now I know this man really knows his stuff!

We jump right back into our discussion of the secret places of Crete his family enjoys. He rattles off names of pink sand beaches where he reminds me to take a bottle to retrieve a small bit of sand to put under my pillow to call in the Goddesses. He shares Matala where the caves in the rock overlooking the sea are so deep that for generations up until the sixties, people lived there full time and then he describes the Preveli Monastery to such an extent, I can hear the monks chanting in my ears.

Marcos is now so enthusiastic that the woman across the aisle asks if she can join in our conversation since she is going to Naxos for the summer and is delighted I will be stopping there on my way to Amorgos for my week of enjoying a sunset that people all over Greece travel to see.

Marcos shares his email and then we both get some shuteye prior to landing. Once on the ground in the airport he reminds me of a Greek God standing tall, smiling wide and reaching to give me a big hug full of satisfaction and joy. With his arms wrapped around me, he says he will look forward to my emails very soon since he is returning to the United States after only one week but looks forward to hosting me at his olive grove on Crete next summer.

Chapter 3
MAGDA

The ferry to Aegina is only 45 minutes from Athens, and you can see both shores at the same time. The excitement on board is contagious and the view is spectacular. We disembark and quickly, the taxis and horse and buggies sweep all of us away to our respective beaches. I am going north instead of south this visit, past the summer Temple of Aphea where we goddesses swim in the cool clear healing water and then brunch under the fir trees, diving into baskets of tasty goodies from Reni's restaurant down the road. My destination is my new friend and poet Magda, who greets me with a fresh loaf of bread from the bakery where she is standing in front, waiting for me with a bottle of wine already in the car and a beautiful smile that only the Greeks share in common when saying hello for the first time. We pile my suitcase into the trunk and take off our required sunhats and hit the road up to the house where she lives overlooking the Sardonic Sea. The red gates, the hanging green grapes, the rosy bougainvillea hugging the walls surrounding the olive groves and the pink house, decked with lovely violet shutters is more of a dream than a reality. I am overwhelmed with excitement of what the sunny days will bring as we hunker down making our plans. The days roll by with swims off the pink volcanic rocks peeking out of the turquoise sea beneath Magda's view, and the evenings are filled with fish, greens, tomato and feta, everything in one of the seaside tavernas, watching sunsets that include fishing boats and mountain peaks. Magda is a published author and poet and is a treasure trove of stories. Her knowledge of Greek Goddess Mythology is endless and her life experience that is shared in her books keeps me in awe. She is 80 but does not look a day over 60 as she zips around town on her Vespa from the 80's in her petite sundresses and big black sunglasses. Her silver hair shines in the sunlight and her energy and enthusiasm for life is contagious. She swims over a kilometer every day from the rocks to the beach as I take the road on foot. Of course she beats me, and then swims back after we spend our chat time on the sandy beach. Nap time is sacred on the island, and as we finish our lunch of souvlaki and beer we head home for the afternoon ritual. Once we revive, the evening begins with ouzo and meze and more stories. The town is waiting, and so are the townspeople of all ages, dribbling into the streets and taverns for meze and music.

 Our morning the next day is spent sewing thin screens together into bags to seal the grapes hanging over the breakfast table from the arbor. These will keep the wasps from eating the delicacies we are waiting for and we sew in quiet meditation. Magda shares her past with me like little pearls attached in one big necklace. Her life is so rich, through triumph and tragedy she goes about her days in an organized serenity of clearing the garden, watering the olive trees, sweeping the marble floors and feeding the animals. When we break for a meal it is always made from her garden and pretty much begins with onions, garlic and olive oil in the bottom of her big iron pan. She makes her own wine, her own olive oil, her own clothes, her own compost pit, writes poetry and novels and most of all educates me on more topics than I knew were missing in my life. Her library is open to me at any time, and the treasure trove of authors keeps me busy between swims, writing and meals.

We visit the local hotels together, always searching for the perfect beach to swim, a bar for a beer and food fit for a Goddess. The best part of Savalla, this small village on the Island of Aegina, is walking. We walk together at sunset along the sea, and we visit Magda's past through the homes she has owned or wanted to own, the neighbors who have known her forever and the beaches and coves she experienced with her children, grandchildren and lovers. My favorite stories are when she gets picked up by suitors from an early age to right this minute. The stories are romantic, colorful and funny. The house is a light terracotta pink with periwinkle blue shutters filled with sunshine streaming through daily and stars peeking through nightly. We listen to the first sea gulls that wake us in the morning to the same putting us to bed at night. We talk about making French toast out of all the bread I mistakenly bought at the bakery, and the homemade noodles she made from scratch during our next meals together. She never ceases to amaze me. When I ask her how she met all of her lovers she tells me it was all about conversation. Striking up dialogue anywhere and everywhere whenever she felt like it. I asked her about the fisherman who she spent 19 years with and never inhabited the same space. She tells me it was all about love and respect. She did not need him underfoot to believe he loved her. He was a sensation at the port and beloved by the other fishermen. He had a job to do and she was reminded of it every day, depending on what fish or not they ate for dinner.

As I offer to do the dishes after our lunch of Greek pilaf, she tells me she had to wash over my dishes from yesterday because we had an omelet. I now find out that egg residue smells, and she washes those dishes with a few squirts of vinegar. Just as she told me, the pilaf must have grated carrots for the sugar, no garlic and a "little Turk" red pepper for the kiss not the bite. The hours roll by with me learning philosophy (what does Magda have to do with my life) and love making when I ask her if her poems are considered erotic. She is taken aback and asks what isn't erotic? Admiring the sea is sensual. Everything is erotic when you are open to the beauty of the land and the people. If the word suits the feeling, that is all. I love this woman. We talk about the Vagina Monologues vs. Arsenic and Old Lace. Our conversations go from memorizing scripts of plays I have been in, to her memorizing her poetry.

How is it that we can remember what we don't want to remember and not what we do? These are the golden kernels of our conversations. She tells me of her lover from France who sails to Greece without ever getting off his yacht.

The descriptions of the food, the light, the people, the art, and the myths are so clear in his mind, she falls in love with his language. How could this man who knows nothing of her culture, paint it in so many awesome pictures? Are all of the men she has loved from a time gone by? Will I have the chance to experience the stories and poems she writes? She tells me about flokati rugs that are hand woven, and teaches me how to pick grapes, prune the grapes and make jam.

We talk of the Goddesses and tonight we are celebrating the biggest Holy Day of the year in Greece, Holy Mary. Men and women are named after Holy Mary and the story Magda tells me is that hundreds of years after the death of Christ, the church was hunting for a female icon for the believers to worship. The patriarchal form of God, being the father, son and Holy Ghost seemed a bit of a stretch for some Christians, and Holy Mary happened to be the perfect fit. Mother figure filled with empathy, compassion and love for her flock.

We sit talking under the stars and listening to the songs bellowing from the village where the revelers are now singing like angels in a choir. I fall asleep with these songs in my ears, knowing it will be all night as they celebrate Holy Mary. We laugh when she shares how to get rid of the hiccups (something she has learned from the local fishermen) by standing over the kitchen sink with a window overlooking the olive grove. She gives me a short glass of water and has me bend over, drinking it from the outer rim. Of course it spills down the front of me and all over the marble floor. Then we move on to leg cramp removal. What to do when lying in bed and the inevitable cramp attacks. She learned this from the folks in her village who apparently had a lot of leg cramps. The secret is to lay flat and take one foot and stretch the toes of the other foot in the opposite direction. Magda's grandmother lived to 110 years old.

Aegina Town is wonderful at sunset. I picked the best seafood restaurant for calamari after a long swim at the beach nearby. The bobbers can be seen from the viewpoint (I was one of them a few hours ago – we bob around in the water with only our heads seen). This restaurant is magical, with my view of the summer temple of Aphaia to my right and to my left, two good looking men playing backgammon and drinking ice coffee. It can't get any better than this. Wait, the view straight out is the beautiful mountains of Peloponnisos, with Athens on the other side.

Today's day at the beach opened with something I have never seen in my life. The Greeks are dripping in suntan oil, sunning to dry from their long swim, drinking ouzo to catch up on the conversations and changing wet babies. The scene is out of a Fellini movie when 6 Chinese women arrive in long dresses, pashmina shawls, and evening gloves covering all the way to their armpits and hats, with veils, hiding their milky white faces. To top it off they are carrying sun umbrellas that are clashing with each other as they bound down the beach, frolicking in the water. Full beards on the men. I haven't seen those since the 70's. I forgot how brilliantly white their teeth are against their dark black mustaches and beards. When I say full beard, I don't mean long; they are full face and neck beards that were around in ancient times. Supposedly, Alexander the Great created shaving, and prior to that, the men groomed their beards for their status. Back to the Chinese women. They are now returning from the sea and their beach walk, and are chattering away as if they discovered Prada. Oh yes, they had Gucci, Prada shopping bags on both arms as they passed by, with smiles as big as the umbrellas they carried

The sun is setting and the golden light is making the sea change to an ink purple with the islands turning into a dreamy foggy remote image of their morning selves. I see the yachts returning from their afternoon sail, with flowing flags announcing their country off the aft. The UK, USA, Greece, Italy and Spain. I am off to investigate the giant white beauties as they are entering the slips at the dock. A flurry of men and women delivering ice for ouzo, squid for meze, and loads of white wine for whenever. The people disembarking are thrilled to be on land, and to enjoy the flavors of the island. The art galleries always have fun artists, poets are reading at the seaside hotels and the jewelry designers have displays that are not to be matched elsewhere. I think about how happy I am when the taverna or restaurant does not have Wi-Fi. I end up writing instead of following facebook. It's addicting, especially when you travel out of the country and want to feel connected to your other life. Forget it, this Greek life is enough for all of us, and once we get into the groove we will never go back. I am speaking metaphorically of course. My life on Aegina takes twists and turns, since I have had more time and experiences here than on any other island. As soon as Magda left for Halandria in Athens last night, her life came alive through the visitors who were calling. First it was Nikio. A handsome man who demanded to know who I was and what I did with Magda. Finally after much back and forth in both languages, his being Greek and mine English, we both agreed we loved Magda but she just was not there.

Next, a few hours later, a well groomed woman, all in white, with loads of stunning jewelry, arrives unannounced and won't leave until I deliver Magda. We have a bigger problem. She speaks absolutely no English and will not consider my Greek at all. I invite Irena in for an ouzo and she accepts. We now have to dance around the conversation, but end up laughing and writing down in code what we want to say to one another.

Chapter 4
KOSTAS & SOULA

I arrived Wednesday night in Crete and do not know where to begin. My hosts, Kostas and Soula, picked me up at the airport. They whisked me away across Crete, through the famous White Mountains, to a breathtaking beach. We hopped on to a motor yacht and joined Stratto and Luna from Cyprus, friends I met in Lemnos. We were all very excited as our Captain; a stunning young man who spoke perfect English, took us past private beaches only reachable by boat. There were coves to be explored and we actually went backwards by boat into a number of them to discover the Cretan light reflecting on the crystal clear water. The mountains are very high at this point and the Samarina Gorge dumps out right where we beached.

The fifth best restaurant in Greece is located on the beach we chose and the swimming is breathtaking. When you walk a few inches into the water, it is way over your head and clear all the way to the bottom. The gorge is very famous. Stratto and Luna's son just arrived to greet us for a swim, after he finished the five hour walk to the bottom of the gorge, which ends at our beach. I must do this walk someday; it is stunning, according to all the folks who eventually arrived. They close the gorge at 2 PM everyday so as not to have too many visitors destroying the environment. How thoughtful! The beaches here are so private that there is nudity, meditation, sunbathing with cocktails and on and on and on. I went swimming and eating.

We arrived back in Chania, the old harbor of the Venetian and Byzantine era, and parked our car at the sea. A bellhop arrived with a cart to push my bags up the hill through town to the family owned Hotel Casa Delfino. The owner/manager is a beautiful young woman named Margarita, and she shares a particular story of the hotel with me. It has been in the family for 6 generations and her father, (God bless him), began the renovation when she was four. She remembers, because she did not see much of him for four years when he was bringing rocks from the sea to create the mosaic in the center of the courtyard, where her aunt (with very big boobs she comments) was shaking out sheets, and the weight of her upper body flung her over the balcony, where the urn stands in her honor today. What stories these Cretans tell.

My room is at the top, and has a marble winding staircase which leads to the giant brick deck, with a view that is about 6 feet across the street into the porch of a couple with beaming smiles and drinking wine. The houses are all over four stories, and because they were built during the Venetian era, are very close together. Margarita's mother, who was an interior designer and now makes meze for the hotel guests, decorated each room to a specific time in history as the family remembers. Very nice. I slept so well knowing the folks across the way were so close and smiling over me.

The next day, another surprise. The city of Chania, with its twisting, curling streets are filled with shops, restaurants and tables. The restaurants are located in caves, on rooftops, along the splashing harbor, and my favorites are in the hidden alleyways, where the locals can be found. We arrive for dinner at Katerina's and already find a group of lively guests, who are all family members, chatting away with excitement about the vegetables

Katerina is picking for the main meal from her garden. We can view the garden from the upper deck of the house where we will dine. Katerina is a well-known wedding dress designer, with 1,187 dresses to her credit, and she is not yet 40. She decided to change careers to become an urban farmer, starting with two goats, 5 chickens and a garden ranging from eggplant to cantaloupe with everything in between. I must also mention the tree house she built with a full bedroom and bath, with the tree going up the center. Katerina made all the food from scratch. The cheese is from the goats, the chicken is from the local farm and the bread is homemade. The evening is so animated with conversation, food and laughter, that I want to do a tour on "The Art of Small Talk". These Cretans have it down. They can talk about cheese until the goats come home!

The next day I am off to one of the officially licensed organic olive oil producers in all of Greece. He is my age and married to a Canadian. Who is managing the operation you may ask, as they always start every sentence with a question here in Crete. The daughter, the third woman in three days, I discovered running their family's company. Chloe is thrilled to hear about "Goddesses Go to Greece" and is going to host a special party for us sitting among the 3000 family owned olive trees. I found out later that the largest percentage of Italian olive oil is from Greece, which is sent in large barrels to be mixed with whatever, and the secret to what the word pure olive oil is.

I also found out that the words Extra Virgin on the label is the seventh most important ingredient; there are six more by which we should be judging our olive oil. Here's a tip, the only oil that is good for us is olive, grape and avocado, in that order.

We leave the olive producer and head to the Number Five best rated beach in the world! Yikes, it is the ancient beach of Pharnarma, and the color is like nothing I have ever seen. The beach is filled with rich Italians who keep it as their secret. There are no bars, no tavernas, no paved roads, just a small cafe where I am going to dine to ancient music and eat stuffed grape leaves. Kostas and Soula are a stunning couple with stories and fun to share all through the day. After returning from the beach, they arranged for me to meet with a brilliant scholar from the University of Thessaloniki, to give me a tour of Chania. The ancient walls, the armory, the churches, mosques and temples, and all the wonderful stories she shared. Just when I thought I would never make it back to the hotel, I was surprised to see a gleaming white carriage with a regal horse of the same coat. We took flight through the streets of Chania along the beautiful harbor with hundreds of tourists gaping.

The next day is the first time we take a public ferry. Energetic Germans, Swedes, and Norwegians, bustling aboard this giant boat with smiles, anticipating an unknown adventure. We glide along the sea, passing uninhabited islands known for their sheer cliffs and crashing waves, and then in front of us is this beautiful white crystal water gleaming in the morning sun. I don't know what to think, when the announcement comes over the loudspeaker, for all those who want to jump over board and swim to land now is the time. Men of all ages disrobe and hand their clothes to wives and friends. My favorites are the Swedes, who look like Olympians, in their red briefs, posing almost as if on purpose, for all the women aboard. The ferry continues on to where we land, at a manmade dock, and hundreds of people disembark into the oasis of natural beauty, large enough for all of us to get lost in our own thoughts and activities. My friend, Soula chooses to lay on the soft pink sand, while I choose to walk in the inches of white water into the turquoise water and then into the warm sky blue waves. It is silent and we are in awe. The beauty of the island overwhelms the guests, as we all strike out on our own, going our separate ways. This is a preserve, as well as a national park, and the only location for water is a canteen with some restrooms. We all brought our own food and libation and not one person leaves a drop of waste behind. The last ferry is at 4 PM since the island actually disappears at 4:15 PM. As we board, the energy is quite different than when we arrived. Quiet, subdued and satiated, we quietly take our seats and listen to the classical music being played, as we move away from the pink sand and tangerine sky.

The next day, the family owned wine vineyard we visit is run by a young woman. The youngest child in a family of boys, her being the only girl. She shares with us her dream of combining her father's wine knowledge, with her background in art, from the University. She is up to speed with her dream. Inside the family home, now turned into an art gallery, cafe and wine bar, she sells us her most popular wine sold in the United States under her name, Alexandra. After a tour of the state of the art wine making facility, Alexandra takes us to the old barn where her grandfather began the business.

There she opens a full kitchen that will be in full swing later this evening. She invited us to the 150 person sit down wine tasting tonight to listen to classical lira and bouzouki. Of course we jump at the chance, since Soula tells me this is not a usual performance and to hear these two instruments together is what drew this huge Cretan crowd, not to mention the wine and homemade Cretan goodies.

Knossos is the palace of the King and Queen of all of the known ancient world 1500 years before the Acropolis was built in Athens. It is said that the King would take his yearly hike up the mountain to get advice from Zeus and then return to manage his flock with wisdom and courage. The palace, in the area near Elounda, Crete, is a large building so intact that one can imagine the daily activity of the dwellers. The Queen's chambers reflect her womanhood and her royalty with painted rose walls and sky blue ceilings. It reflects a woman who spent a lot of time dressing. There is a dressing room, a bath, a makeup room and a toilet. The King's chambers reflect his power. It is larger than the Queen's and has an antechamber, where there are rows of seats against the wall, where men and women would wait for an audience. I understand it was mostly about money, according to what the archeologists could make of the writing on the walls. To me, the most interesting part of the palace grounds is the theater. An amphitheater of about 500 seats carved out of stone, with a long marble walkway beginning at the edge of the palace walls. I can just imagine all of these people waiting in line for a good seat

Back in Chania, right near my hotel is Agora. This is a cross-shaped building filled with cheese, olive oil, vegetables, fish, meat and honey stands. A big bazaar of everything Cretan, with restaurants, bars, clothing, stalls of fine leather shoes, belts and purses. We head for a kitchen filled with tables, where the cooking is in full swing 24 hours a day. I am amazed at the swiftness of the chef, the son of the old man, who seats us and serves the traditional first course of raki. Mom is standing on a ladder under a giant wine barrel, filling the copper tins of wine. The son is now making the traditional moussaka with an eggplant base. He is combining olive oil, rice, tomatoes, and cheese in a giant pot and mixing it with his arms! I jump up from my table to get a photo of this extraordinary cooking skill, when a man across the room yells for me to wait. I am so startled that my camera flies out of my hands into the pot and brings down the house in screams of laughter. The good news is the camera dried out and of course we made friends with the culprit. I find out through our long lunch of Cretan horta, cheese pie and loads of white wine that this is the only restaurant that is open 24 hours a day because the unique soup helps drinkers with hangovers. During the night the Agora is closed up tight, and the backdoor to this place is known to be open for a cure for a night of drinking. The place has a genuine musical sound that I cannot describe. Remember this is where Zorba the Greek hung out.

Chapter 5
THALIA

The island of Lemnos is a treasure unknown to most Americans and filled with surprises on a grand scale. Arriving at the Hotel Ephelia, a magnificent stone country house, filled with antiques, wine and happiness, I found myself speaking to a renaissance woman of great passion, intrigue and grace. The owner, Thalia, returned to her grandfather's land and built this hotel by herself with stones from the sea where the hotel sits in all of its glory. Thalia has retrieved these stones one by one on her daily diving expeditions and also from the ancient hillside where the donkeys and goats roam. Thalia has even built the road that leads the guests to their suites, which includes in the design, her mood of the day. It's sometimes a sailboat or sometimes a seashell.

To know her is to love her. Who wouldn't love a woman who bought a tractor and cleared her own land in this day in age. She fills the entrance way with flowers and herbs and sparrows who nest above the outside garden rafters on their annual trip from South Africa. She reminds me of my sister back in Athens. Nothing is a mystery. Chantal will make the Greek version of paella before

8 AM for the afternoon lunch, just as Thalia serves a tasty dish of goat, potatoes, tomatoes, zucchini, eggplant, carrots, red and green peppers all from her own garden in front of the hotel. We eat homemade feta cheese on homemade brown bread, with sweet figs from her fig trees, while she reveals the history of her family. Thalia shares the history of Lemnos as we ascend to our suites with magnificent views of the Bay of Moudros. I am told that during World War I, there were over 200 ships on their way to Gallipoli from the same view. The rooms are all handmade stone with huge bathrooms and soft and beautiful curtains and pillows, all from her grandmother's dowry chest that she began at the age of fourteen and finished at seventeen, when she married. The lamps were made by Thalia, with intricate herbs glowing from yellow glass, that makes the atmosphere actually feel ancient.

The island of Lemnos is known for introducing the first Parliament in Europe, and the Paliochni is one of the two most ancient in all of Europe. There are 31 authentic villages, all with their own personality and many have their own wine. The wine from Lemnos is ranked among the best in Europe and from the Muscat grape.

We head down the mountain with our tour guide Jasmine, which means healing in Greek, to an ancient spa. This is the most mesmerizing spa I have ever visited, with byzantine doorways and Venetian ceilings with incredible colorful natural lighting. The treatment I received took place on a slab of turquoise tile in a marble and stone room. The mud of Terra Lemnia was used in ancient times as a medicine for a number of ailments. After my session, I glowed like a candle and that night at dinner, the other guests were so impressed with my radiance, men and women got up to go to the reception desk and book whatever treatment I had that day. The beautiful Lemnian women who run the spa are trained in a specific ancient massage that releases toxins and rejuvenates the face, a beauty secret of Ifestia, the word for Lemnos in ancient times.

Wherever I visit on the island, I find Lemnian women who are running businesses and creating art. I ask Thalia why the women on Lemnos are so powerful, and she immediately responds "because they are loved". The men on Lemnos respect the women to such a degree that they are given whatever they desire.

We head to a sustainable farm where the hostess Irini is going to give us a cooking lesson, using every ingredient from her own farm. She is a beautiful blonde woman who has a charming farmhouse with dishes, art, pots and pans and most of all a giant copper distillery in the center of her kitchen. Irini prides herself on her homemade liquor, tsipouro, and presents us with three tall colorful glass bottles of it with an assortment of small glasses for tasting. We are now sitting comfortably around a welcoming wood table and begin our afternoon of conversation, eating and laughter. Irini explains to me that Lemnians believe in the art of discussion, and the food and tsipouro are there to enhance the interesting dialogue. We feast on Irini's homemade marinated sardines, barley bread, tzatziki, feta cheese, capers, olives, edible flowers sunflower seeds, pesto, tomatoes, cucumbers with salt from the local salt lake, and then the finale, quince and pears with Petti Mezzi, a homemade syrup that is sprayed on the fruit like aromatherapy. When we finally get up to say goodbye, Irini apologizes for the meze tasting and invites us for a real lunch tomorrow, and hopefully she will see us in the evening in the village of Mirena, where she owns Irini's Art & Jewelry Gallery.

One of the oldest theaters in Greece features a yearly Greek Theater Festival in the fall and is in the middle of the countryside where carved out of the rocky hillside there are seats for 2000 attendees. There is one marble chair for the King or Queen when one of them shows up late for the performance. The theater is located nearby the Temple of Artemis from the 7th century BC, where there's a pre-theater considered the broadcast center of ancient times where the news of the day was delivered to the community. The Temple of Artemis overlooks a cliff with a view of the sea, which includes the sea cave of the general, who was left behind by Troy's army and was sheltered by the women of the Temple. The climb down to the cave is worth it, and the story is shared by the town's people with great enthusiasm.

The island of Lemnos is known for its poets and was celebrating at the time of my visit the 100th Anniversary of a Poetry Conference, which I had to experience for myself. I started out on foot and reached a beautiful white wood house which is unusual for the Greek Islands. I did not see anyone outside as I approached, so I inched my way up the tall steps and opened the screen door. I swear the scene was something out of a movie. The room was large and filled with beautiful Victorian furniture with a small bar in the corner which I noticed only served brandy. The entire room was quiet and filled with men and women seated in dainty chairs and petite velvet sofas. What surprised me the most is they were all wearing white. The women were wearing formal white dresses, some full length and beautiful and the men were wearing white linen suits and ties and bow ties. The rustic environment with the backdrop of the sea is a cornucopia of creativity the Lemnians tell me as writer workshops flourish. Whenever I compare the island of Lemnos to the island of Naxos with all the European vacationers, motorbikes and action. I think about what my friend back in the States always says, "nothing wrong with that!"

Chapter 6
IRINI

The island of Amorgos is such a delight it takes my breath away, 5,000 years old and showing it in its ancient beauty. Giant rocky mountains surround the bay with tiny white villages sprinkling their steep sides.

The moon came up from behind one of them last night during our dinner taking place on a massive patio hanging over the sea. What a night of laughing, eating and storytelling. Irini, my host, is the owner of the Aegialis Hotel and Spa, a family owned hotel, originally built and managed by her ancestors. We have many friends and family members join us throughout my stay to share with me their own personal stories of the island, and its healing and rejuvenating properties.

25,000 goats with big bells around their neck greet me wherever I go. Each goat owner knows their own bell's sound and it is intriguing to hear the music of these bells throughout the day. The dinner table consists of a mix of personalities and I am enjoying hearing each colorful story as they unfold throughout the evening.

The doctor from the village joins us and shares that he is a specialist from Athens who chose this island to practice for its beauty and even though he is the only doctor on the island, he will take care of all its 2,000 inhabitants. He chooses to eat salad and fruit since his wife is joining him from Athens and she has not seen him in four months. Irini, who is the quintessential Greek Goddess, with the black flowing hair, the dark olive eyes and soft Mediterranean skin with few lines, although she complains she has little ones around her mouth because she smiles a lot, has been joined by her husband, Nikita, who is quite handsome, with his rough tan, his work clothes from the day of tending to the landscape and his smile instead of conversation. The daughter arrives and of course is tiny, slim and priestess-like in her movements and charming when she tells the story of the mystery behind the water of the island of Amorgos. The myth of the Goddess Kirki, known as the temptress, used magic on her conquests in addition to her beauty. I don't know if it is a coincidence but there are an unusual amount of beautiful women on this island.

There are many sites throughout Greece that feature a triangle. Sites that are geographically apart from each other, like the Parthenon in Athens, the Temple of Aphaia on the island of Aegina and the Temple of Sounion at the southernmost tip of the country. Here too, there are sites that are the exact kilometers apart from each other forming a perfect triangle. Irini says the energy field from the triangle and the extreme depth of the surrounding sea creates the "Lalon Idor" which means healing water or talking water. The "Nuls Zias" crystal is found here and it cleanses the body of any trauma and uplifts the spirit which connects a person to their true source.

The evening always starts slow and late, and the food comes out of the kitchen even slower. This gives us the opportunity to talk about our day and taste the vegetables that are grown beneath the hotel, which are all organic, even the olive oil. Meze is served and begins with greens called vita that look like kale but are crunchier, and an ouzo. I share how I spent my day going to two monasteries. One that is 1,000 years old and is built on a side of a cliff that takes forever to walk up the steps. Once at the top I am welcomed by an Orthodox monk dressed all in black as he sat against the stark white walls. He offers the traditional candy and sends you further up the steps inside the ancient walls.

The view from the monastery rooftop takes my breath away. I am alone with this monk who followed me in silence and offered me a glass of tsipouro. I head down the steep stairs and I'm on my way to visit the next monastery. This one has an entirely different vibe. It has been reopened and restored after 400 years, two years ago by a young nun. This is the monastery of St. George where an icon of him was found in the water beneath it. She does not believe that the healing miracles come from him, but the fact that Amorgos is a spiritual source due to its location on the planet and the occasional shifts in the plates of the earth on both sides of the island. Irini tells the story of people who have been healed with problems of muscle pain, depression, addiction, and difficulties with bones.

I head to the capital of Chora, where out of all the tavernas on the island I choose one that is owned by a true Goddess. Soula and I are meant to meet. She also tells me about the healing powers of Amorgos and why women from all over the world come here for treatment of fibromyalgia, osteoporosis and depression. The taverna she owns is decorated with a very feminine touch with white chairs and paintings of the seaside everywhere. Other women are now joining us for a wine or coffee and I notice they are all very beautiful. I am stunned. I can't keep my eyes off of these women of all ages. Soula notices my surprised look and comments that because of the minerals in the water of the island of Amorgos the women are beautiful. The minerals in the water clean the blood as they flow through the pores and take out negative ions and replace them with positive ions.

This is the second time I hear this beauty tip. The first, is when

I was having a rejuvance facial massage at the spa that Irini insisted I try. This unique massage from ancient times is taught in Athens and is a finger face massage. It takes place on your face with fine little finger pinches that affect all the nerves and muscles in your body. I could feel the energy going down my arms and through my legs and out my feet. The masseuse explains the illnesses we hold in our face are from our entire body, and once released even the lines on our face disappear. Yikes! She was right. I noticed this when I was preparing to go to dinner this evening.

Irini and I have been friends for years and her hotel is one of the best in the Greek Islands. The indoor Goddess swimming pool features a black and white marble checkered floor with tall white arches. The yoga patio hangs over the sea and is draped in willowing white sheers. A Goddess trip to Amorgos is worth its weight in diamonds. Speaking of diamonds, that is what the water looks like as it changes hews all day long. In the morning, it is crystal white, in the afternoon it turns turquoise, and in the evening it is a violet silver. Every evening, when sitting down to dinner with my new found friends here at the hotel, we discuss the water and its color and its minerals and all this conversation takes us into discussions of ancient Greek history and of course mythology.

Last night Irini and I walked up the slope of the mountain to her family village, where there are 126 residents. It is an ancient village with twisting streets with the white and blue doors featuring the smiling faces of the octogenarians, mostly her family. We end up at a taverna joining her aunt and uncle who are having their dinner in the kitchen. Grandma is washing the dishes and is not even looking up from her task when we say hello to her. That is why she is 93 and still going strong at midnight! Uncle is a poet and is eager to find my Goddess and what makes me Claudia. He only speaks Greek and has a smile as big as his overflowing mustache. At the end of the evening, saying our goodbyes, Uncle presents me with a poem written on the order pad of the restaurant. Three long pages that were later translated for me by my Greek nephew and something I will treasure for the rest of my life.

So few Americans and British come here that I found only one English language book in the library. Around the pool during the day, I hear French, German and Italian all day long. The Norwegians and the Swedes are the most fun at our nightly beach parties, where a small boat with a big bucket of meze and drinks whisks us away to a remote beach for a sunset swim. Upon arrival on the sand we all dash into the sea for the last swim of the day before nightfall.

My final evening in Amorgos I am introduced to two Baronesses. One from Switzerland and one from the United Kingdom. Amorgos is their favorite island in the entire world, and one of the women has had a home here for over 23 years. The Baroness, who has a house here, is intrigued with my cheap bracelets from a souvenir store at the port, featuring the evil eye. We discuss the myth behind the evil eye and it is said that it keeps you protected from jealous people from sucking your energy. The Baroness, who has the house in the village, invites us to dinner and as we climb the slope to the village I realize we are back at Irini's uncles and he is very happy to see us. As we are seated at the best table in the taverna overlooking the busy square, the music begins with two handsome young men playing the lyre and the bouzouki. Baroness, who has a house here, tells the story of a young man. He is in love with her daughter, who is a well trained classical violinist, and she is presently on a world concert tour. The young musician has a limited education and is a shepherd. I find that love has its problems no matter what part of the world we live in.

Chapter 7
MARIA & ALESSANDRA

My two favorite Goddesses and new friends are in their late 70's, and still vibrant, vital and exciting. I met them both at a dinner at the King George Hotel in Athens on New Years Eve and they invited me to lunch the following week. Both are very beautiful and both very interesting. They shared that they were friends for over 30 years and both were married to men who were 30 years older than them. Both of their husbands are gone now, which leaves them to their own charm and diversion; they have a new business venture they want to discuss with me. I love these Greek women. Always open to the new, and always appreciative of the old. It's like their skin. They may be old, but their skin is in a constant state of new. It's that Mediterranean diet and of course, the white wine.

Prior to my arrival at Maria's apartment, my research tells me that she lives behind the Parliament, which was the Royal Palace. I mean literally, the street is in the backyard of the Queen's Garden from the old days when royalty reigned. I found out, from my very sophisticated brother-in-law, Spiros, that I must call the Parliament security to make sure I can walk down the street, since it is a private street and guarded at both ends by the gorgeous Evzone guards dressed in their white shoes with the pom poms on their shoes. I let them know an approximate time of arrival and begin my walk to the Parliament. I was so impressed with the striking architecture of the buildings on this street, I anticipate an interesting afternoon. All the way down the street, one building was more beautiful than the next, especially the gardens overflowing from every sun filled balcony.

I was buzzed in and sent directly up to the Penthouse where Maria was waiting for me. It's 11:30 AM, just in time for an aperitif before lunch at 2 PM. It's customary in Greece when having a lunch date. The apartment is stunning, with a garden patio overlooking the National Gardens. The photos on the walls and tables reflect a time gone by. The hunt, the palace, the horses and of course Maria, beautiful in her riding breeches. One photo of her is in Madison Square Garden, New York City, where she competed in an international horse show with her horse that was trained by the Royal Guards in England. We enjoy having horses in common, and we share equestrian stories over cocktails. Maria takes me to the small servant's kitchen, reaches deep into the ice box for cubes, slowly counts them out and places them with a long silver spoon into two tall crystal glasses. Maria tells me she takes her cocktail tall and I tell her so do I. We toast to our new found friendship and begin our journey through her lovely nest she calls home. She shares with me the reason there is no dining room, and why there is only one small servant's kitchen. Maria and her late husband had such a busy social calendar they did not eat at home nor entertain at home. There were private clubs for entertaining and cafes for dining with friends of course, who insisted on their company on a regular basis. What a wonderful life. Because of her social standing due to her late husband, Maria is able to garner friendships from all over the world, in addition to those she made in Greece. After her husband passed, she went into the power broking business and asked her pal Alessandra to join her. They help people get things done. They assist in cutting through the government paperwork, the bureaucracy, and most of all the chain of command. For this they make a pretty nice living, and this helps cover the expenses of their island villas.

    Maria explains to me that she and Alessandra have a lot going on in business, and would like to discuss this at lunch. Off we go, arm and arm, down this incredible street, past the Parliament police like two school girls who have a secret pal they are eager to meet for lunch. We arrive in Kolonaki Square (the Madison Avenue of Athens) at one of the best cafes in the city, where the seen and hope-to-be-seen are dining. I understand from my brother-in-law, Spiros, that it is very important where one sits. So, I am keenly observing the next move Maria makes. The maitre d' opened the middle glass door which takes us to an open air patio filled with beautiful people. To the left there is a cafe that is a bit more casual, and to the right are distinguished men smoking cigars and drinking tsipouro. We stay in the center and are guided to the best seats in the house. This table is in the rear of the cafe, in front of the enclosed restaurant, which is filled with a giant chandelier reflecting red and gold walls. The table was made for people watching. The lovely banquet filled with comfy silk cushions told me it was going to be a lengthy and enjoyable lunch and I was right. All eyes are on us and especially on Maria's full length white linen pantsuit and the blinding diamond on her finger she carries so well. The observers were obvious. Young couples dressed in the latest designer clothes, chatting on their cell phones and young men smoking and pretending not to notice us, but just the same, taking a peek now and then, with brimming smiles. Darling Alessandra arrives in a flurry, speaking Greek throughout her entrance to anyone who would listen. Alessandra is short, dressed in all black, and looks a bit like Coco Chanel. She insists we rearrange our seating so she can smoke without bothering us, and calls to the waiter to move quickly. To my surprise, they ordered a small bottle of exquisite Greek wine for me, and a Greek Mythos for Maria and a Heineken for Alessandra. They love beer and even drink it out of the bottle. These elegant women with their beer in this over the top luxurious restaurant made me smile from ear to ear. It was a fantastic moment and a scene I will never forget. I knew at this moment we were in for a fabulous afternoon. The stories flow, the guests at other tables join in, and there is laughter as well as a tear or two. We talk about husbands and careers and what we want to do when we grow up. I knew then I wanted to share my experience with these two women, with all women. I felt so empowered, and to discover these two lovely women, who knew how to bring out their Goddess in such a delightful and radiant way. I knew this was the beginning of an important journey, and one I was sure was going to be a nice ride.

My first genuine surprise was Maria's invitation to her summer home on the island of Spetses, known for its birthday cake mansions and horse-drawn carriages. There are no cars allowed and every house is managed and taken care of by a charwoman. I was so excited, talking about all of the schemes we will cook up during the upcoming summer on Spetses, I didn't even notice it was dark outside.

Chapter 8
MELINA MERCOURI

As a woman in transition, while on a trip to Greece to find my inner Goddess and discover who I really Am, I happened upon the era of the 60's frozen in time in an Athenian boite.

A boite is a poetry lounge-cabaret the beatniks crowned for wine and words of revolution and romance. Joined by my friend Rhoda from South Dakota, it all began with our search for Melina Mercouri's cafe, where the writers, poets and actors come together for gossip and lively discussion. It serves a delicious meal and fine wine. It is not on any tourist map and is off the beaten path in Plaka. I always begin at the top of the Acropolis and make my way down to remember the direction of the street where it is hidden. As I circle the low road around the Acropolis and with one right and one left, the cafe welcomes us with open doors and beautiful Greek music. Upon entering one is overwhelmed with the giant photograph of the exceptionally lovely actress Melina Mercouri and with a closer look we see the walls filled with the photos of famous actors from all over the world who sat and sang at these small cafe tables snuggled together for intimacy and lively discussion.

Rhoda and I decided to sit next to the most interesting group of people we could find and there, sitting in front of us, was a stunning woman who looked like Melina Mercouri. She was blonde and had on a beige suit, beige pumps and had a beige purse and was just so gorgeous. I couldn't resist asking her a question. We wanted to know who she was and what she was about. I said, "excuse me, are you a writer?" And, she said, "a poetess". I felt like I was in a Greek movie from the 50's and Melina Mercouri was going to walk through the door as the main character. She smiled and ordered us both a fabulous white wine and we chatted some more about the cafe. It turns out the writers who are published frequent the cafe like in the 60's, before computers, to get inspired, to drink and eat, to talk and most of all to be surrounded by other artists for creative and political discourse. People were speaking in Greek, French and German and having lively debates on topics of the day, like mythology, politics, music and art. The discussions included anyone who wanted to participate, even us.

Enter Heros. A Greek God for sure. He looks right out of central casting, with shoulder length coal black hair, a mustache to match Salvador Dali and a handsome sculpted square jaw, which reminds me of the statues we just viewed at the Acropolis museum.

Heros pulls up a chair and invites himself to dine with us and explains he owns the art gallery next door. We do not put up a fuss and we enjoy each other's company. Heros suddenly realizes we truly are interested in the Athens art community and want to know more about how and where we can continue this wonderful afternoon with such a creative and dynamic crowd. It gets better. We pay the bill and walk out arm in arm with Heros, this time like a Fred Astaire movie, up the slab stone streets, through narrow alleys with tiny doors, and then a tall marble staircase. Up the staircase we go, when Heros finds a mysterious door and knocks on the sliding glass window. Nose to nose, he is facing another Greek

God named Yiannis, his friend. Yiannis looks us over and slides the door open to reveal a setting which struck me so I thought I was in a dream. A beautiful woman in a red gown with long black hair playing the cello and a young man playing the piano in an almost spiritual manner. It was dark and they were surprised to see us. I felt I was stepping back in time and they were people I knew in another lifetime. What Goddess could this be and was I then? Coming back to reality, Heros tells us we will be returning this evening without him but Yiannis will be waiting for us. The Greeks eat their main meal in the afternoon around 2 PM and late in the evening they go out for a meze (light snack) with a glass of ouzo or wine. This makes so much sense to me since it seems so much more social and non intrusive when listening to music or song.

 We had our meze at 8 PM at a traditional taverna in Plaka with Greek dancing and enjoyed the locals appreciating their own fine dancers. Two men and one woman got up from different tables, strangers who took command of the dance floor. A jaw-dropping sight. The three danced together with passion and style and their synchronized movements were impeccable that even the singer on the stage was in awe. Checking our watches, we pay our bill and head for the boite. Up the staircase, down the alley, the two of us walking hurriedly, anticipating an adventure. We find the staircase, the hallway, the sliding door and then, I am nose to nose with Yiannis, who looks even more like a Greek God in the dark. He scoots us to two seats that were reserved for us in this packed house. The room has over a hundred guests and people are sitting everywhere on small rope stools with small wood backs. The group is sitting in a U with a tiny cocktail table in the middle of the room filled with tall glasses of Olympia wine. It is red wine with water added, this is like what was served in ancient times we are told. Yiannis sends us two shot glasses of tsapporo and I warn my guest not to drink it and that she pretend it is too strong and pass it on to our new young friends we have just joined. This group was thrilled with our generosity as the tsapporo kept arriving all evening plus our Olympia wine, courtesy of absent Heros.

Young hipsters, guys and gals, grandmothers and grandfathers, uncles and aunts, students and us all enjoying the music. What a wonderful blend of talent, as we all sing along to the piano player singer who led us in the words of songs of days gone by, when Greece was struggling. Everyone in the room, except us, knew the words and sang with such verve the walls echoed and made for a joyous evening. The beautiful woman, who played the cello, now took to the stage to sing old well known Greek romance songs, complete with responses from the audience. What struck me as fascinating, was that no matter what the age of the guests, they all knew the words to the songs, which made it all the more inviting to join in as a fellow (fake) Greek. Surprise, Heros appears on the stage and to our delight, is reciting poetry of Greek writers from ancient times right up to Greece in the 70's.

Heros is so handsome, committed and passionate and we are so proud of him. Our new friend and there we were participating in his big moment. The crowd loved him and recited his poems back to him (it must be a Greek thing) and of course we chimed in loving every minute. I turned to my pal and not to my surprise her jaw dropped, being from South Dakota, she never experienced anything like this and of course, the ancient Olympian wine added to the excitement. We ended up being the last to leave.

Chapter 9
ATHENA

As I walk up the hill along the sea, thinking about Aphaea whose seaside temple I am now visiting in my Greek swimsuit and my Goddess sandals, I wonder who the women were whose footsteps I am walking in from ancient times. I know they were probably smaller and perhaps carried their prepared lunch like I am, but were any of them blonde and blue-eyed like me?

I wear my evil eye around my neck, given to me by my sister. Chantal says the evil eye protects oneself from anyone who is talking about you behind your back or is jealous of you. She says beware of someone who is complimenting you too much.

All the questions I have to find my inner Goddess are now erupting in my psyche as my mind seeks ancient answers on this morning's temple pilgrimage.

My favorite time of day, since I am an early riser, is the morning. Greeks are late nighters and the tourists are too, so I have an advantage of having the Temple to myself this morning. I have my lunch packed by Athena and think about which Goddess she is most like. Athena is so supportive of me, although we do not speak a word of the same language; we are bonded together as Goddesses. We are alike in age, life history, challenges, independence and tenacity. Our mutual respect for each other reflects the ancient times when women empowered each other. True Goddess friendship is cultivated when women are communicating from their hearts and minds without a single word spoken between them. When I am with Athena, I have an overwhelming feeling of comfort and peace. I don't want to forget a morsel of the generous portions of insight my Goddess (whoever she is) is blessing me with right now. I am determined and ready for a day of introspection, sunshine and prayer, swimming under the Temple of Aphaia on the island of Aegina. I am so caught up with my plans and the heavenly scenery ahead of me, I hardly notice my new little pal at my ankles. A Jack Russell Terrier, one of my favorite dogs. While he yelps, I ponder where he came from and also my new relationship with Athena. I believe people come into each other's lives for a purpose, the purpose being to help each other grow towards their best potential. It's at this moment I wonder how many more people I would meet to help me on my quest for my inner Goddess and my best potential.

 I settle in on the white stone sand with my new dog participating in my ritual as if he were my own. I name him Apollo and walk toward the water and slowly emerge into the turquoise sea. My mermaid Goddess tells me to lie on my back and float with nothing in my mind, not to think about anything and feel like there is nowhere to go. I peer over my elevated toes and see Apollo sitting straight up, soldier style, watching my every move. Apollo, the protector, fills me with a sense of security. I fantasize that the Goddess Aphea will appear soon as my oracle, and share with me some profound advice. I now take this opportunity to emerge from the sea, never drying off. Greeks never dry off and only use a beach towel if they are wearing it. I climb on to some giant rocks underneath the temple and Apollo joins me. I decide we should have a morning prayer and focus on gratitude. My prayer concentrates on the glorious gift I have been given, to experience this mystical ruin right at the exact time I am experiencing my personal transition. I concentrate with my eyes closed and begin speaking my personal mantra out loud.

I was chanting quite loudly since no one was around. I am chanting in appreciation for my gifts while Apollo is watching me with curiosity. He is relaxed and I can tell by his beautiful eyes he is very happy. After a few minutes, I realize there is an echo coming from beneath the temple on the other side. I am intrigued and want to know if it is my Goddess chanting back to me some desired advice. But, almost at the same time I relax in that thought, I hear the chanting get louder and louder and it sounds like more than one person. Is this Goddess speaking, I ask myself?

I begin chanting in response to the chanting I am hearing, and then suddenly, silence. I look at Apollo and he looks at me. In the silence, there is a voice that breaks it, and it's a woman and then we hear another woman.

It sounds like Goddesses to me. They are both calling out the name, Apollo, and my little pal goes running toward them. Apollo takes off running on the rocks on the beach and happily returns to his proper owners who were thrilled with his safe and happy return. I figured they were the owners, but to my surprise, they were also the Goddesses who were chanting on the other side of the temple at the same time I was chanting, therefore the echo. I fall into a comfortable communion of hearts and minds, without a single word spoken, we understand each other. Their body language and their hand signals tell me they were my echo, chanting the same mantra at the same time under the Temple of Aphaia. The two women Goddesses told me with their gestures that Apollo probably never felt lost because we had the same vibrations through our mantra that he recognized a fellow follower.

These sweet, delicate Greek women, invited me to pray with them every morning at the Temple of Aphaia, while I was visiting the island of Aegina; we even brought Athena along for a chat and a chant.

Chapter 10

KATERINA

Katerina is sitting alone at sunset at my favorite restaurant in Souvala, a town on the island of Aegina. It resides on a side of a cliff with the view of Athens across the sea, where we can only imagine the heat and the teeming crowds.

The sun is about to set, and the few guests left over from the lunch crowd are tossing their leftover bread into the sea, while we all watch some unusual fish gobble it up. I am alone at the table talking to an expatriate who I thought may be interested in talking with me after a frantic email message. To my dismay, instead of saying how wonderful it would be to be sharing the islands of the Cyclades at sunset, he is looking at his cell phone.

This incident reminded me why I was in Greece alone. Since I specialize in women traveling alone, I peruse the patio and find a couple of women, I ask the first one where she is from, and without a smile she says Germany. I move on to a woman who looks like she is in another world. I try the same question, and with a smile she says Northern Greece. She beckons me to join her with a generous gesture. I pick up my glass of wine and sit down at her table, where there are remaining sardines, tzatziki and calamari. I am relieved the German woman turned me down, and am happy to learn my new friend speaks English. We talk and talk. Her name is Katerina and her husband was killed in a car accident. She travels alone and will never go back to any destination she went to with her late husband. Katerina loves the idea of my Goddesses Go to Greece Tours for women, and tells me she also is a woman in transition and says she feels she will always be. Another total stranger pouring her heart out to me, about the burden of figuring out how to live a life alone. She is beautiful, blonde and strong. She works for a company that sells technology to the United States government and wonders if she may soon lose her job. Katerina shares with me her political viewpoint of the past economic crisis in Greece and feels it is Greece's own fault. At the same time, she quotes the United Kingdom's study that says that Greeks are the second hardest working people on the planet. We ponder this statement together. She feels that the Greeks should examine their government's constitution and place in the world, before making judgements about local politicians, and how they got into the now settled economic situation and the EU. (European Union) We talk about how the European Union makes comments on the number of houses a Greek family owns, always a minimum of two or more. Katerina tells me the Greek culture takes care of their children first, no matter what.

Houses are the family homes, and if you don't have one, you are not taking care of your children's future and their children's future. The Greeks work very hard to maintain this tradition and it is unable to comprehend a German or United States point of view. In the United States, we flip houses and look at houses like the stock market, a mere investment. The Greeks consider houses as a safety net for generations to come, and are rewarded for this thinking by the love of their children who take care of them in their aging years. Greece has so few assisted living centers, caretakers or retirement homes. Greeks live with the children for whom they provided the houses, and the houses are the safety for generations in the future.

Katerina and I talk about marriage and children and both of us have had husbands but no children. She is about fifty-five and feels she will never marry again. The times have changed, she says, and we cannot trust people as we did before the internet. We don't know what men want from us anymore when it comes to a relationship at our age. Money, sex, family, business savvy, friends, caretaker or just someone to hang out with. Who are they and where do they come from, Katerina asks.

We talk about women traveling alone like no other time in history. She says it's better to be somewhere alone that will receive you graciously, than be with someone with whom you feel alone. I love Katerina for her candidness and her ability to articulate in her new found English language the perils women face from all over the world. Katerina and I have agreed to have dinner the following night, after she looks at her watch and sees two hours have gone by. She compliments my company and looks forward to another evening of conversation and laughter.

Chapter 11
YIANNIS & ANASTASIA

Yiannis and Anastasia own a large bustling, bright white taverna overlooking the sea at the best beach in Souvala, located on the island of Aegina, where the most in of the in crowd of Souvala hang out. The backgammon games are in full swing among the men and gossip is more important to the women. I joined the bar crowd and set up my ipad computer to check my emails. It's a small comfortable bar of only 5 seats so I am soon alone with Facebook. The bartender starts dancing to the rap music he has just turned up and serves me a small draft with a shot of tsipouro. Oh boy, he is handsome and colorful and full of energy. Dark hair, dark tan, dark eyes and brilliant white smile. We fall into pleasant conversation after he finishes pretending he doesn't speak English. Yiannis is his name, and he is not the bartender, he is the owner and a documentary journalist for the 60 Minutes TV show of Greece called the Time Machine. Yiannis explains to me that Time Machine is more in depth than 60 Minutes because its priority is history and stories and biographies that are all served up in a lengthy series. Greeks like history and they like to spend a lot of time thinking and speaking about what they are watching instead of being fed someone's point of view. Yiannis was one of 250 journalists fired when TV ERT let go 2,500 people out of 4,000. He feels strongly that he is a journalist and it does not matter if he is employed. He will investigate and report on his own and find companies to feature his documentaries. He is a true entrepreneur and enjoys not being rich. He has enough to fill the needs of his family and believes journalists that are rich are suspect. I say, no kidding, after reading in the UK newspapers that the average TV journalist - Anchorperson at ERT made over a half a million dollars a year. Enter Anastasia, Yiannis's lovely wife. She resembles the American actress Faye Dunaway and is proud of it. Anastasia has been working as a political journalist for 19 years and has been able to survive the recent debacle. She goes online and shows me the TV company she works with and the news team. It is very much like the United States in that everyone is over the top beautiful and everyone is speaking at the same time in loud and aggressive voices. For some reason, this presentation of the news seems to work in Greece, better than the United States. Anastasia's story of a career woman in Greece, her challenges as a mother (the little monster just ran by screaming at the top of his lungs) and her life married to a man with a wandering eye. This is where I can relate. She is beautiful and fragile as she shares with me her vulnerability. I believe it is because I am a stranger and she has been waiting a long time for my arrival. As her back is turned, minding customers and the little one, Yiannis shares with me that he was with an American woman before Anastasia, and that is how he was able to buy this taverna. The American woman showered him with gifts and money and then he never saw her again. He believes she was living out some sort of fantasy and there was no need to complicate each other's lives.

 Anastasia returns with the news that her salary was cut two-thirds. We talk about the perception the world has of Greece and its past economic crisis. We talk about the recent study that has been recently presented by a research company in the United Kingdom that states Greeks are the second hardest working people on the planet and the most vilified. It doesn't matter how hard they work, the world still sees them living in paradise and are lazy. The world is jealous. I feel this way about Hawaii.

The evening crowd is rolling in, still wet from the sea. Everyone looks lighter and sexier and happier than this afternoon. The ouzo is being served and the music has changed from American to romantic Greek and technology and backgammon has been put away. Conversation, laughter and meze are now flowing with ease like the sun setting into the sea.

The nighttime full moon of August is very important to Greece and the Moon Goddess is taken seriously. The darkness of the night when the moon is at its most glowing is the backdrop for the live concert that I stumbled upon on my way home from the beach side. The music is compelling and inviting as I turn the corner and to my delight I see a woman in a black evening gown, with long black hair singing traditional Greek songs accompanied by an electric piano. I am alone with about four people and feel the concert is being put on just for us, when I make a sharp turn and on the other side of this hillside are about 1000 people seated in the dark, quiet like the night, listening in awe to this beautiful Moon Goddess.

The Moon Goddess is especially important on the island of Aegina and also on the island of Lemnos. The many olive groves usually were where there was a spring, often in a grotto, where the water trickled out of a rock. I experienced this event on our visit to the Temple of Artemis with the women from the village. They took me on a trail hike into the woods and underneath the many olive trees, there were trickling springs everywhere. These springs, it is said, are the healing waters where the priestesses washed after fasting and meditation, prior to their yearly visit to the Temple to access the wisdom of the Goddess Artemis. Some say that this magical ritual is paramount to accessing our unconscious mind and assists in giving women a roadmap into their own psychological makeup, behavior and moods and the power to alter any of it.

Chapter 12
VASILIKI

The Greek Islands seem to all have their own official rooster, who crows every morning at the same time and lifts one from a sound sleep. The Greeks, who go to bed very late on vacation, seem to sleep through it, but not me. The sun is beginning to stream in through the closed shutters and it is getting very difficult to ignore the brilliant light of the new day on the island of Aegina. So many mornings I desire to sleep in and review my dreams of the night before or have some of those short important morning dreams. But no, it just never works out that way. While visiting my friend Sophia she introduces me to the island way.

Today's schedule includes a walk up the rocky coast to visit Vasiliki to pick basil. Sophia decided last night we were going to make pesto today and fresh basil is in order. Every morning, after deciding the evening meal, we walk about to find what friend or neighbor has what herbs we need and what we can barter for. We decide on walnuts from our own tree for Vasiliki and we would also put walnuts in the pesto. Vasiliki runs one of the loveliest hotels on the island of Aegina and grows all the herbs in the garden of the hotel grounds. It's funny how the Greeks pronounce herbs as the man's name Herb's possessive.

Vasiliki runs a nine room hotel, makes her own jam, creates special events for her guests, from cooking classes to yoga classes. Her son is in charge of the yoga, which is a big hit with the women, her husband mans the bar and grandma washes dishes to keep busy and make sure the kitchen staff keeps busy. As I eat my final Greek salad (no lettuce thank you) on the island, I reflect on my ten days here and all of the colorful characters, who added to my life. I remember the dreams (symbols of power, horses, water, temples, books) and my interpretation of them with my new found friends. Their take from ancient times and the Goddesses and mine from modern times living in California. It's difficult to spend a day without a swim no matter what time. The sea changes color with the light so there is a constant reminder of change just as our lives change and we embrace it or we don't. The Greeks have an uncanny ability to change with the times, they are survivors and lovers of life. They quote invasions like songs and victories like flowers in their garden.

Sophia made sardines last night in tomato sauce and told me her sister broils them in a small oven. I suggest a toaster oven so they don't completely shrink. She disagrees. She fries eggplant slices in sizzling homemade olive oil that she douses in a thick flour crust. The tzatziki is nothing like mine. She shreds the cucumber, insists on garlic, adds a small amount of feta and includes yogurt. We dip our toasted bread (that I bought too much of the other day and she toasted it to save it) and it has a real punch. There is something about cooking in Greece that makes food taste better and I believe it is all the conversation that goes into it during the shopping, preparing, cooking and eating that it is always the main experience of the day.

At one of my favorite restaurants, which I love, the men come in one by one to join large tables of conversation, laughter and meze. They entertain each other with no technology and have laughs from the heart and tears from the soul. I like the fact that I don't understand a word they are saying, it is music to my ears to just feel and hear the intonation of their voices vs the actual words of their conversation. The air here makes everyone beautiful. No one wears face makeup, as far as I can tell, including myself, it is so freeing. Maybe a dab of eye makeup when we go to town or out in the evening, but that's it. We are natural Goddesses and proud of it! There must be something about the Mediterranean diet. The way one can eat the same meal every day. Now I do. I do not research ethnic food, designer food, healthy food, craving food, or sugar (Greeks do not eat big desserts like Americans). There are no Chinese, French, or Italian restaurants on the islands (maybe Santorini and Mykonos for the tourists) but the authentic Greek Islands where the Greeks live and holiday, there is not one sushi bar or taco stand. My nephew, Theodore's crowd in Athens do the cocktail circuit. They always say they are going out for a cocktail. They think it's one drink and it's international and American so they drink a gin and tonic, whiskey sour or margarita.

    Sophia told me last night during dinner that in Greece no one removes the plates from a table even in a fine restaurant because it means the evening is over. That is why you can never find a waiter when it is time to pay the check. They honor the time you have spent in their restaurant and want you to go away remembering it and wanting to return. Once plates are removed it is a sign to hurry up and leave. They do not have the concept of turning the table like in other countries, including the United States. Time for conversation, laughter and eating is more important than turning a table. Children are welcome and they dine with their parents, friends and grandparents. Someone is always paying attention to them and they do not do themed restaurants to placate the children. They spend their entire meal on the attention of the children, how wonderful they are, how great their stories are and what they will do tomorrow. No technology and no nannies. No need for babysitters.

Today, while swimming, I noticed a fishing boat pulling into the port. One of the women around me swam over to the boat and said something to the people on board in Greek. After finishing her swim she arrived at the boat where they handed over a bag of goodies. Now that's what I call fresh fish.

I am dining at my favorite restaurant on the sea. It takes me over an hour to eat my Greek salad. Now I have moved on to the horta, the lovely greens that are in season this time of year. I am alone with my thoughts and my writing and I see the sea changing once again in the light. I want to change as the sea does. I want my life to reflect the light on the sea. I will go for another swim soon with this idea in mind. The sea has changed since I have been having my afternoon dinner. The water is sloshing now as most Greeks are home dining prior to their afternoon nap. The heat of the day starts about 2 PM and lasts until about 6 PM. This is when I write. It is so quiet even the dogs are sleeping.

Chapter 13
TEMPLE OF APHAIA

I arrived by ferry with my sister and her close pal from the United Kingdom in search of the perfect place for me to rest my head tonight and enjoy my first Goddess alone experience on a Greek Island. The island Aegina is surrounded by the azure blue sea and is host to the Temple of Aphaia. The beautiful seaside inn is waiting, and once the cozy beachfront room is booked, we head by taxi to our favorite taverna with the famous Greek blue and white tables and chairs that sit in the sea. We relax the afternoon away, drinking white wine and eating many small plates of Greek delicacies served in the water by a young Greek God named Stavros. He runs back and forth to the taverna from the sea and fills our plates as they go empty after each swim.

I talked about my desire to start my personal quest for my inner Goddess with Aphaea and doing it alone the next day. We all agreed it was best to start early and spend the day alone to get the full effect of the Temple of Aphaia.

The next morning I arrive by local bus to the Temple of Aphaia, and since I am the only passenger I am alone. As I am climbing up the marble stairs to the temple I notice I am not alone as I expected. One man and me, together pacing through the Temple in the quiet of the morning. He is a Muslim. He has on a long white robe and small white cap. He is black and beautifully tall. We see each other and acknowledge each other with a nod. We began to avoid each other on purpose out of respect and allow each other the space needed to absorb our own experiences.

I am here to find my inner Goddess and he also looks like he's on a mission. It is mysterious and lovely at the same time. Two of us spent over two hours walking, sitting and meditating in different areas of the temple. I will always remember the silence. The beauty of knowing I was sharing my experience with a stranger from a far off land and feeling so close to that person. This is what I believe is the shared experience of the universe. We are all one but never notice. I had a lot of time to notice this day and make a promise to myself I would notice more, especially people and the experience I have had with them. It is like a slow heavenly dance.

I know the tourists will arrive soon and I do not want them to change my mood, so I gingerly climb down the rocks surrounding the temple and cross the street to a cafe. Again, I am alone and find a bar serving coffee. To my delight, there is a garden in the rear of the bar with large ancient stones as tables and seating. I cannot decide where to sit because the view from each table is more beautiful than the next. One is a view of the sea with flowers falling from above to the crest of the shore. The other is a view of the temple, with the light of the day blinding me. I am certain I will never leave. I know if I sit and write I will be lost there for the rest of the day. I decide then and there I will make a commitment to each Goddess on this adventure in Greece and the Greek Islands to discover who she is and what she accomplished and most of all how she coped. I want to connect with Goddesses who are powerful and courageous and who will help in my personal transition to a woman of wisdom, without fear of the future and most of all to be one hundred percent responsible for myself.

THE END

GREEK FAMILY RECIPES

BY
CHANTAL KIELICH KAKOLIRIS

Recipe Table of Contents

1 YEMISTA (Stuffed Tomatoes and Green Peppers)
2 PERCH
3 SPAGHETTI BOLOGNESE
4 SKORDALIA (Fried Cod and Garlic Mashed Potatoes)
5 PORK CHOPS (With Broccoli and Rice)
6 SPANAKORIZO (Spinach and Rice)
7 KRISTINIA (Wine Sticks)
8 KOTOPOULO ESTRAGON (Chicken Tarragon)
9 CANAALONI (Stuffed Tube Pasta with Ground Beef)
10 PRASSA (Golden Leek Tart - Leek Pie)
11 BAKED WHOLE FISH
12 BEEFSTEAK-STO-FOURNO (Salisbury Steak with Potatoes)
13 SPANAKOPITA (Spinach Pie)
14 ORANGE/CARROT BREAD
15 SOKOLATA
16 LEMONI CAKE
17 TIROPSOMO (Cheese Bread)
18 KOURAMBIEDES (Easy Christmas Cookies)
19 SOUTZOUKAKIA (Ground Meat Sausage)
20 THENDRA TREATS (Greek Dog Cookies)

YEMISTA
Stuffed Tomatoes and Green Pepper

Ingredients:

⅓ lb. Ground Meat
4 Tomatoes
4 Peppers (green and yellow)
8 TBSP Rice
2 Potatoes peeled and sliced
1 Garlic - clove crushed
½ Grated onion
1 Cup Olive Oil
Salt - Dash
Pepper - Sprinkle
1 Tsp Dill

Preparation:

Slice off the bottoms of tomatoes and scoop out insides
Place in bowl
Cut off the caps of peppers and scoop out the insides and discard the seeds
Sauté ground meat with crushed garlic and onion
Mix all remaining ingredients together in mixing bowl
Stuff each tomato and green pepper with a toothpick
Place in baking pan with sliced raw potatoes
Pour an inch of water over the entire dish
Add a circle of a arm's worth of olive oil (put your arm straight out and create a circle motion above your pan drizzling the olive oil)
Sprinkle with sea salt
Bake at 425* for 1 hour

PERCH

Ingredients:

2 Large filets of Perch
Rosemary - Pinch
2 TBSP Olive Oil
Lemons – sliced
Paprika – sweet - Dash
Vegetable of your choice

Preparation:

Line pan with tin foil
Place fish in pan and add a circle of an arm's worth of olive oil (put your arm straight out and create a circle motion above your pan drizzling the olive oil)
Add the rosemary
Place the sliced lemons on top of the filets
Sprinkle with the sweet Paprika
Cover with tinfoil (make a tent)
Steam a vegetable
Bake at 425 for ½ Hour

SPAGHETTI BOLOGNESE

Ingredients:

Linguine or spaghetti
Mushrooms
1 Clove Garlic - crushed
Oregano
1 Bouillon Cube – Vegetable
Pepper - Dash
Ground Meat – Turkey or Chicken
2 TBSP Olive Oil
1 Cup Tomato Sauce

Preparation:

Boil the pasta at the same time you are preparing the sauce.
Slice the mushrooms and sauteed in olive oil
Add the crushed garlic
Add a pinch of oregano.
Add 1 vegetable bouillon cube.
Add a dash of pepper.
Add the ground meat, turkey or chicken
Add Tomato sauce
Simmer in pan for 20 minutes on medium fire and serve on top of linguine or spaghetti

SKORDALIA
Fried Cod Fish and Garlic Mashed Potatoes

Ingredients:

2 lbs. Cod Fish
1/2 Cup Flour
Vegetable or Corn Oil
2 Potatoes
1 Clove Garlic - crushed
1 Tsp Vinegar
Olive Oil - a few drops

Preparation:

Heat until hot - Vegetable or Corn Oil
Dip Cod Fish into Flour and coat on both side and dredge
Add Cod Fish to Vegetable or Corn Oil
Fry until golden brown and flip to other side
Place on Paper Towel to drain oil
Serve with Potatoes
Boil 2 white potatoes and mash with butter, crushed garlic and add 1 teaspoon vinegar
Add a few drops of olive oil on the fried Cod Fish and the Mashed Potatoes

PORK CHOPS
Pork Chops with Broccoli and Rice

Ingredients:

4 Pork Chops
Mushrooms
2 TBSP Olive Oil
1 Bouillon Vegetable Cube
2 Cups Rice
Pepper - Dash
Thyme - Dash
1 Cup Broccoli

Preparation:

Add olive oil to pan
Brown Pork Chops in Olive Oil on both sides
Slice Mushrooms
Add sliced Mushrooms to pan
Add Thyme
Add Pepper
Add Vegetable Bullion Cube
Add Rice
Add Broccoli
Bring ingredients to boil then
Simmer on LOW for 45 Minutes

SPANAKORIZO
Spinach and Rice

Ingredients:

2 lbs. Spinach - fresh
½ Cup Long Grain White Rice
1 Small Onion - chopped
1 Garlic Clove - crushed
¼ Cup Parsley - chopped
2 TBSP Dill
2 TBSP Olive Oil
1 Vegetable Bouillon Cube
1 Lemon
1 Brick Feta - crumbled

Preparation:

Wash and drain spinach
Heat oil in large pot
Saute onion or garlic
Add rice
Place uncooked spinach on top
Simmer until spinach is wilted
Add all other ingredients
Continue cooking until all liquid is absorbed
Turn off heat and let rice simmer
Add feta on top and serve with lemon wedge

KRITSINIA
Wine Sticks

Ingredients:

½ Cup White Wine
½ Cup Olive Oil
1 Tsp Salt
1 Tsp Sugar
2 Cups Self-raising Flour
Seeds – sunflower, sesame, poppy

Preparation:

Add flour to the mixing bowl and mix then add all the other ingredients until doughy.
Take one inch of dough and roll between the palms of your hands into a stick.
Place on an ungreased cookie sheet.
Brush with olive oil
Add seeds or nuts as a topping
Bake at 350 for 10 minutes or until golden brown

KOTOPOULO ESTRAGON
Chicken Tarragon

Ingredients:

2 TBSP Tarragon
2 Chicken Breasts
Salt - Dash
Pepper - Dash
2 TBSP Olive Oil
1 Vegetable Bouillon Cube
1 Cup Flour for dredging
1 Small Carton Cream
1 Cup Sliced Mushrooms

Preparation:

Slice chicken breasts into small pieces
Dredge in flour
Heat pan with olive oil
Add bouillon cube
Add salt and pepper
Add crushed garlic
Add mushrooms
Add small carton of cream
Add chicken breasts
Simmer for 30 – 45 minutes until tender
Serve with Pasta (green noodles)

CANAALONI
Stuffed Tube Pasta with Ground Beef

Ingredients:

1 lb. Ground Beef
1 Garlic clove - crushed
1 Cup Cheese - grated
2 TBSP Olive Oil
2 Handfuls Mushrooms - sliced
1 Cup Tomato Sauce
Salt - Dash
Pepper - Dash

Preparation:

Heat olive oil with crushed garlic and salt and pepper
Sauté ground beef
Add sliced mushrooms
Scoop ingredients into uncooked tube noodles
Place in glass baking dish
Pour tomato sauce of entire dish
Sprinkle grated cheese on top
Bake at 350 for 1 hour
Serve with grated cheese

PRASSA
Golden Leek Tart - Leek Pie

Ingredients:

4 Leeks – medium size
¼ Cup Vegetable Oil
1 TBSP Olive Oil
½ Stick Butter
3 Eggs
Pepper - Pinch
Dill - Pinch
1 Cup Milk or Cream

Preparation:

Prepare pie crust or buy ready made
Cut off tops of leeks (cut where light green meets dark green)
Chop into small pieces
Sauté leeks in olive oil until soft
Mix together eggs, milk, dill, salt and pepper
Place leeks in pie shell
Pour mixture on top
Bake at 400 for 30 minutes

Light lunch for the ladies with a glass of white wine!

BAKED WHOLE FISH

Ingredients:

1 Large Fish - Whole
Rosemary - Pinch
Thyme - Pinch
Basil - Pinch
Oregano - Pinch
Dill - Pinch
1/2 Cup Olive Oil
1 Lemon - sliced
Salt - Dash
Pepper - Dash

Preparation:

Line pan with tin foil
Pour olive oil in pan
Place fish in pan
Sprinkle top of fish with herb of your choice
Place Lemon slices on top of fish
Wrap fish in closed tinfoil like a gift
Bake at 350 for 1 Hour

BEEFSTEAK-STO-FOURNO
Salisbury Steak with Potatoes

Ingredients:

2 lbs. Ground Salisbury Steak
½ Loaf of stale Bread or 4 slices of Toast
1 Egg
Oregano - Pinch
Salt - Dash
Pepper - Dash
½ Onion - grated
1 Clove Garlic - crushed
3 TBSP Olive Oil

Preparation:

Soak bread in water
Add all ingredients to bread
Knead the bread with the meat
Form into small patties
Add olive oil to baking dish
Place patties into baking dish
Bake at 350 for 1 Hour or until brown/flip at ½ Hour

SPANAKOPITA
Spinach Pie

Ingredients:

2 lbs. Spinach
1 lb. Zucchini
1 Cup Yogurt
2 TBSP Dill
1 Egg
1 Brick Feta
1/4 Cup Olive Oil
Pepper - Dash
6 Sheets Filo

Preparation:

Steam Spinach
Steam Zucchini
Drain Spinach and Zucchini
Squeeze out excess water
Pour olive oil in pot used for steaming
Smash Feta in Olive Oil
Add Yogurt
Add Dill
Add Egg
Add Pepper
Chop Spinach and Zucchini
Add Spinach and Add Zucchini
Spread 4 sheets of Filo in baking pan
Spread Mixture into Filo
Place 2 sheets Filo on the mixture
Bake at 425 for 1 Hour and Cool before serving

ORANGE/CARROT BREAD

Ingredients:

1 Cup Sugar
1 ½ Cup Self-raising Flour
½ Tsp Salt
2 Eggs
½ Cup Orange Juice
4 TBSP Vegetable Oil
1 Cup Carrot - grated

Preparation:

Mix all ingredients together
Pour into loaf pan
Bake at 350 for 1 Hour
Cool before serving

SOKOLATA
Chocolate Cake

Ingredients:

1 ½ Cup Self-raising Flour
3 TBSP Cocoa Powder
1 Cup Sugar
¼ Cup Powdered Sugar
5 TBSP Vegetable Oil
1 Cup Cold Water

Preparation:

Mix ingredients together
Pour into baking pan
Bake at 350 for 30 Minutes
Shake Powdered Sugar on Top

LEMONI CAKE

Ingredients:

6 TBSP Vegetable Oil
1 Cup Sugar
1 ½ Tsp Grated Zest - Lemon Peel
1 ½ Cups Self-raising Flour
1 Cup Milk
2 Eggs
½ Cup Walnuts (optional)
½ Cup Confectioners Sugar

Preparation:

Mix all ingredients together
Bake at 350 for 1 Hour
Top with Juice of one Lemon and sprinkle Confectioners Sugar

TIROPSOMO
Cheese Bread

Ingredients:

2 Cups Flour
1 Tsp Salt
½ Cup Water
½ Cup Feta
2 TBSP Mint - chopped
1/4 Cup Olive Oil

Preparation:

Mix all ingredients together
Form into small patties
Fry in Hot Olive Oil
Cool

KOURAMBIEDES
Easy Christmas Cookies

Ingredients:

1 Cup Butter – softened
1 Cup Confectioners Sugar
½ Tsp Vanilla Extract
1 ¾ Cup Flour
½ Walnuts - finely chopped

Preparation:

Mix butter and sugar
Add Vanilla Extract
Mix
Add the Walnuts
Form into ball
Refrigerate for 1 hour until firm
Pinch off an inch of dough
Roll in hand
Place on ungreased baking sheet
Bake at 350 for 15 minutes
Cool
Roll in Confectioners Sugar

SOUTZOUKAKIA
Ground Meat Sausages

Ingredients:

1 lb. Ground Beef - lean
4 TBSP Olive Oil
1 Garlic Clove - crushed
½ Cup Wine
1 Egg
¼ Tsp Sugar
1 Cinnamon Stick
1 Tsp Cumin
1 Can Tomato Sauce
2 Tsp Parsley – finely chopped
1 Vegetable Bouillon Cube
1 Bay Leaf
Salt - Pinch
Pepper – Ground – Pinch

Preparation:

Prepare ground meat with salt, pepper, egg, and cumin
Knead all together
Roll in sausage form – roll with hands
Saute in hot olive oil until brown
Add all other ingredients to the pan
Ccook for 30 minutes
Serve with a steaming grain dish or mashed potatoes

GREEK DOG COOKIES
Thendra Treats

Ingredients:

2 Cups Flour
1 Cup Feta Cheese - crumbled
½ Cup Carrot - shredded
1 TBSP Olive Oil
1 Splash Water

Preparation:

Combine flour, cheese and carrot
Stir in Olive Oil
Add water as necessary to make stiff dough (dribble water)
Pinch ½ portion of dough between hands
Place on un-greased cookie sheet
Bake at 250 for 1 hour or until thoroughly dry (crunchy)

About the Author

Claudia Kielich is a resident of Los Angeles and Athens, Greece and is a Virtuoso Luxury Travel Advisor owning her own company Goddesses Go to Greece, which features customized specialty travel, designed for travelers interested in the authentic lifestyle of Greece.

After years of worldwide travel in a career in live entertainment for Radio City in New York and Universal in Los Angeles, Claudia took her extensive knowledge of travel to the next level by taking advantage of visiting Greece and the Greek Islands for over 20 years.

It happens that her sister married a Greek and began a traditional Greek life, sharing it with Claudia through family, food, fun, culture, daily traditions and especially the Greek people.

Claudia's unique Goddesses Go to Greece Transformational Trips for Women take place seasonally for her guests to enjoy the festivities of the traditional Greek Holidays.

Copyright © 2023 by Claudia Kielich

Cover by Eberle Arts

All rights reserved.

No part of this book may be reproduced in any form or by any electronic or mechanical means, including information storage and retrieval systems, without written permission from the author, except for the use of brief quotations in a book review.

Printed in Great Britain
by Amazon